**Nominated for 3 EISNER AWARDS including**
**Best New Series and Best Ongoing Series**

**Featured on the Best of the Year List**
**for The Village Voice, IGN and The Oregonian**

"Incredibly fun and ridiculously addictive. . . A roller-coaster ride through a library, weaving famous

authors and characters into a tale of mystery that is, at once, oddly familiar yet highly original."

**-USA TODAY.COM**

"Cas          and intelligent, engrossing from the first page, THE UNWRITTEN is a gem

          iracy story with enough metafictional layers to launch a thesis or two."

**-SCRIPPS HOWARD NEWS SERVICE**

hriller that slyly plays off the real-world mania for imaginary ones . . .

t only created a brisk and addictive story, sketched with crafty allusions to

e, but also neatly subverted the celebrity-worship manias of fantasy fandom

and questioned the very nature of storytelling itself."

**- PUBLISHERS WEEKLY**

"A High-Minded Literary Hodgepodge-with Wizards!"

**-PORTLAND MERCURY**

"A top-tier reading experience."

**- IGN**

"Fascinating."

**- BOSTON HERALD**

"Everything I love about comics, period."

**- AIN'T IT COOL NEWS**

"Favorite book of the year."

**- NEWSARAMA**

the
Unwritten

Karen Berger SVP-Executive Editor
Pornsak Pichetshote Editor-Original Series
Bob Harras Group Editor-Collected Editions
Robbin Brosterman Design Director-Books
Louis Prandi Art Director

**DC COMICS**
Diane Nelson President
Dan DiDio and Jim Lee Co-Publishers
Geoff Johns Chief Creative Officer
Patrick Caldon EVP-Finance and Administr
John Rood EVP-Sales, Marketing and Busin    opment
Amy Genkins SVP-Business and Legal Affairs
Steve Rotterdam SVP-Sales and Marketing
John Cunningham VP-Marketing
Terri Cunningham VP-Managing Editor
Alison Gill VP-Manufacturing
David Hyde VP-Publicity
Sue Pohja VP-Book Trade Sales
Alysse Soll VP-Advertising and Custom Publishing
Bob Wayne VP-Sales
Mark Chiarello Art Director

SUSTAINABLE
FORESTRY
INITIATIVE
Certified Chain of Custody
Promoting Sustainable
Forest Management
www.sfiprogram.org
Fiber used in this product line meets the
sourcing requirements of the SFI program.
www.sfiprogram.org PWC-SFICOC-260

# the Unwritten

## Inside Man

Mike Carey & Peter Gross  Script - Story - Art   Jimmy Broxton Finishes – Jud Süss

Kurt Huggins  Zelda Devon Finishes – Eliza Mae Hertford's Willowbank Tales

Chris Chuckry  Jeanne McGee  Kurt Huggins  Zelda Devon  Colorists

Todd Klein Letterer  Yuko Shimizu  Cover Artist

THE UNWRITTEN created by Gross and Carey

# Introduction

*The Unwritten* is Mike Carey and Peter Gross writing literature, in two different ways. Firstly, in that, for instance, the story of a French regional prison governor who loves his fantasy-prone children is not one that sits within a genre. It's the sort of thing, like the existential plight of Tommy Taylor, one would expect from a novel found in the middle of the book store, not at the frayed edges where books whose characters live within sets of reader expectations hang out. There's no format: the stories here all contribute to a bigger tale, but we're not waiting to see what our hero and his friends will get up to on their quest this issue. They might not be in it. Or they might be, but it might not be about them. Carey and his co-plotter/artist have created a literary playground for themselves out of thin air. There's a central mystery about what's going on, but the digressions and notes in the margin are just as interesting.

This is almost an anthology, of stories bound together purely by theme. But it's such a huge and compelling theme that there's no good reason why anyone should ever want that mystery to be solved.

That's the second way they're writing literature: obviously, they're writing *about* it.

They want to show us the gravitational distortion of reality by fiction. For instance, when our heroes encounter a phantom version of Nazi brutality, they just about ignore it initially, the *Raiders of the Lost Ark* or *Cabaret* theme musics probably playing somewhere in their unconscious. They're not too perturbed by it: they think they've seen this, that they know what this is. It's to the creators' credit that they find a new way, with the tale of *Jud Süss*, to shock us with the fascists' own distortion of reality and text. The background radiation of *The Unwritten*, as seen in internet forum and blog snippets, is a psychotic real world one degree more hysterical than our own, weighed down by fiction, shaped by it almost to eschaton, or as science fiction writers would have it, to the point of singularity. The title of the series itself might refer not to something that hasn't been done, but to something that's being undone, a tapestry that's being unpicked.

*The Unwritten* also uses the language of magic to talk about literature. *Willowbank Tales* exists not only to have fun with sweary rabbits, but to describe the negative space within stories in a magical/psychological way. That space is represented by a literal vault of the unconscious. (I'm sure we might soon meet a madwoman in an attic.) *Jud Süss* is rendered into a cosmic monster, something out of H.P. Lovecraft or P.J. Hammond. A missing creator writes between the lines in novels, in the details. That feels like something a schizophrenic might tell you. Narrative equals consciousness equals magical power equals political power, an

equation which feels instinctively true, which might even define existence.

Amongst all this, Carey and Gross don't neglect character. 'Mr. Bun felt like a clock that has been over-wound.' A horrible fate for those undeserving of it that doesn't feel like something one would normally find in fiction, but that instead speaks of reality. An untrustworthy but charming fellow traveller who's actually a writer himself, but never quite describes himself as such.

As I said: doing literature while talking about it. It's like we're watching them pull themselves up into the air by their bootstraps.

## Paul Cornell

*Paul Cornell is a Hugo award-nominated writer whose television credits include* Dr. Who, Primeval, *and* Pulse.

### The Fall of Tom Taylor???
*POSTED: Wednesday, October 21 @ 12:00 am*

*Now how art thou fallen from Heaven, oh Tom Taylor, son of the morning!*

Don't get me wrong. I know these are hard times for all quasi-celebrities, with the public attention span running shorter than ever; and the wise old proverb tells us that there's no such thing as bad publicity. But I think our boy Thomas is testing that theory to the limits.

Tom's claim to fame was always a little dubious, to be honest. Okay, so his father wrote the most popular series of books the publishing world has ever seen: and yes, Tom shares a name (more or less) with the young wizard who stars in those books, Tommy Taylor™. But really, Tom is not that interesting a guy, and his sole contribution to the legend was to earn a meager crust on the fan circuit signing his father's books.

Then he hit the news when an earnest young lady challenged him at a convention, claiming that most of the documentation relating to Tom's so-called life is forged. Cue howls of outrage, crazed denunciations, burnings in effigy — and then, more surprising, the emergence of a cult who believe that Tom IS Tommy, the word made flesh, a multiplatform savior for a media-saturated age.

That might have been something of a happy ending, if Tom hadn't then gone to the Villa Diodati — the last place where his famous father was seen alive — and (allegedly) slaughtered half a dozen people in an insane and possibly drug-fueled orgy of violence.

What else? Mysterious cabals? Shadowy assassins? Unconfirmed reports that a winged cat was seen flying over Geneva on the day of the killings? The rumor mill runs on hard fuel, kiddies. It can't grind smoke.

This entry was posted on Wednesday, October 14 at 12:00 am. Tags: **Celebrity, Pop Culture, Arts and Life.** You can skip to the end and leave a response. Commenters must abide by the forum's Rules and Regulations.

To France's borders the columns came:
To a high pass, Roncevaux its name.
"Rejoice," said Roland, "ye Christian thanes.
The air you breathe blows from France's plains."

Dust hid the road, and the sun's fair face.
"See," said Sir Oliver, "for God's grace.
It is the king, I swear and trust.
A great host raised these clouds of dust.

"We have found our brothers in arms again.
Together we'll say farewell to Spain."

A host indeed, in good array.
The Pagan army bars their way.

Four hundred thousand men, or more:
Never saw Earth a larger store!

"In mighty strength are
the Heathen crew,"
Oliver said, "and our
knights are few.
Roland, I beg you,
sound your horn.
The king will hear,
and his host return."

"Now God forbid it, for very shame,"
Said Roland. "I would be to blame
If out of fear I called the king,
His arm to bend, his aid to bring.

"Olifant, my horn,
shall here abide,
Untouched, unsounded
at my side."

"Twice ten thousand
    he gave to me
And they are a goodly
    company.
No coward heart,
    no traitor soul
No stain upon
    this muster's roll.

"Let the heathens come,
    and let them fall.
As God shall please,
    we'll cope them all.
And if we die,
    'tis holy ground.
Who dies for Christ
    in Heaven is
        crowned!"

Fearless, too, are
    their Pagan foes.

Frenchman and Saracen,
    thus they close.

# INSIDE MAN

...THE UNLAWFUL *MURDER* OF MATHILDE VENNER, JAMES MORTENSON, LAUREN SEDGEWICK, SIMON GROVE, SONIA TAFT AND STANLEY EARL JARDINE.

PAS COUPABLE.

A LITTLE *LOUDER*, PLEASE.

I SAID *NOT GUILTY.* NOT GUILTY ON ALL COUNTS.

I DIDN'T *KILL* ANYONE!

IF IT PLEASE THE COURT, THE *DEFENSE* WILL CONTEND--

LET'S NOT *PREVIEW* THE DEFENSE, MADAME SCHIEL. THIS IS AN ARRAIGNMENT, NOT A TRIAL.

SIEUR, THE *VICTIMS* AT THE VILLA DIODATI WERE FOR THE MOST PART AMERICAN OR BRITISH. BUT MATHILDE VENNER, THE HOUSEKEEPER, HELD A *FRENCH* PASSPORT.

THE FRENCH *COUR SUPÉRIEURE* HAS THEREFORE APPLIED FOR THE EXTRADITION OF THE DEFENDANT, THOMAS TAYLOR, SO THAT HE MAY BE TRIED ON FRENCH SOIL.

SERIOUSLY? THE FRENCH WANT TO LAY *CLAIM* TO THIS MULTIMEDIA SHIT-STORM?

IT SEEMS SO, SIEUR.

CIEL! THEN WHAT ARE WE *WAITING* FOR? THIS IS LIKE A BLESSING FROM *HEAVEN.*

THE JUDICIAL *AUTONOMY* OF OUR SISTER REPUBLIC IS RECOGNIZED.

I AM REFERRING THIS CASE TO THE CANTONAL COURT, FOR A SUMMARY *TRANSFER.*

AS OF NOW, *TOM TAYLOR* IS SOMEBODY ELSE'S PROBLEM.

# Dr. Swann Cares about YOU

ONLINE PSYCHIATRIC HELP FROM A CERTIFIED PROFESSIONAL

Home | Help Me | Helped | Special Features | Store

GO!

**Q.** Q: I tried to keep my daughter Sarah from finding out about the Diodati murders, but someone at school told her and then she read something in a chatroom. Now she just won't stop crying. I've tried to explain to her that Tom Taylor isn't Tommy - that it's a coincidence that they have the same name. But she knows that this piece of filth is Wilson Taylor's son. She even met him once, and had her photo taken with him. It's honestly like a rape. She's been abused, not physically but still very genuinely. I don't know how to make her trust the world again.

Lily Frears,
Cape Cod

Dr. Swann answers,

**A.** I can see how much pain this is causing you, Lily, and I suspect that this is a situation that's made you feel like an abuse victim, as well as your daughter. If it's any reassurance, I do believe that you've started well, by establishing the difference between reality and fiction and making it clear that the one doesn't influence the other.

Of course, the situation is complicated here by the fact that she has actually met Tom Taylor. There are, if you like, two different traumas to deal with here, and they're both profound. Sarah must feel frightened and confused at the thought that a man she met and spoke to, and gave her trust to, has now been accused of terrible, indelible crimes. And at the same time, she must feel as though the fantasy worlds that she builds for herself -- as every child does -- have been tainted and made unsafe by the presence in them of Tommy Taylor, who is of necessity associated in her mind with the alleged murderer Tom Taylor.

Your patience and love will both be of vital, central importance in helping Sarah to disentangle these two things and convincing her that it's safe to dream again. If the dreams of a child are a garden, she must believe that she can play in that garden without fear, without foreboding. Right now that might seem to be an impossible task, but children are resilient and they can recover fully from terrible psychic harm.

I'm going to divide this process into three phases, and take you through the key factors belonging to each of

ive
'a'Doc
the book
oks
l Listings
rviews
Studies

---

I don't even think it's about the killings. Okay, they're terrible, and yeah, he should stand trial for thej, but what about the other stuff? What about what he's done to the world? It's like genocide. Tom Taylor is the Eichmann of our times. I want to see him tried inside a glass box.

Back to top | profile | pm

**JanMaryBellows** · Posted: 10:19 pm | quote

But the glass box was to protect Eichmann. So I guess you'd rather see him tried without a glass box?

Back to top | profile | pm

**Mirrorman** · Posted: 10:52 pm | quote

Okay, yeah, I see what you're getting at. No glass box.

Back to top | profile | pm

**PoohBear** · Posted: 11:05 pm | quote

But do they know for sure he did it? They didn't have a trial yet. Hard to know how the trial could be fair now, because everyone hates him so much. Weird. Last week we couldn't get enough of him.

Back to top | profile | pm

**STANIS12** · Posted: 11:18 pm | quote

He was the only one still standing in a house full of dead bodies. And he wrote a story about what he was going to do. They found it. It was Tommy Taylor torture porn. He pretty much signed a confession.

Back to top | profile | pm | www

**Mirrorman** · Posted: 11:43 pm | quote

You know that's up on the net? They keep taking it down again, but if you use Webcrawler and type in "twitching mass of skinless tissue," you'll find it.

Back to top | profile | pm

**STANIS12** · Posted: 11:44 pm | quote

He'd better hope they find him guilty. If he ever gets out of jail, I give him a week, tops, before someone whacks him.

Back to top | profile | pm | www

**Mirrorman** · Posted: 11:59 pm | quote

Slowly. It's got to be slowly.

---

HOME PAGE | TODAY'S PAP

# The News Ti

WORLD | U.S. | N.Y. / RE

AFRICA | AMERICAS | A

---

## Come to Judgment

By VINCENT J. HAMMER

SIGN IN TO E-MAIL
PRINT
REPRINTS
SHARE

ARTICLE TOOLS SPONSORED BY
茶を飲む

Controversy continues to surround the murders at the Villa Diodati in Geneva, and the subsequent police investigation. Diehard Tom Taylor supporters claim that the evidence which led to Taylor's arrest was circumstantial at best, and that the police have failed to follow up on reported sightings of another man in the vicinity of the Villa in the immediate run-up to the brutal killings.

The Villa Diodati became a true site of gothic horror this past week.

But as the forum for Taylor's trial shifts from Switzerland to France, fewer and fewer voices seem to be raised in his support. Local chapters of the Tommy Taylor Fan Club throughout Europe and America have ritually "divorced" themselves from the troubled celebrity, many of them tearing out Taylor's autograph from treasured copies of his father's best-selling novels.

Even more extreme responses have come from other sources - including a record number of direct threats to Taylor's life from outraged former fans, some of which are under active investigation by the police.

Taylor's aberrant behavior in the past few weeks has been seen by many as a response to an incident at London's recent TommyCon. Taylor was confronted by a graduate student who accused him of not being who he claims to be, asserting that most of the documents proving his identity are forged.

Taylor went to ground, but was pursued wherever he went by enraged and disillusioned readers of the beloved novels. He was then hospitalized after an incident in which he was kidnapped by an obsessive fan dressed as Tommy Taylor's fictional nemesis, Count Ambrosio. The incident culminated in the detonation of a nail bomb, killing Taylor's stalker but leaving him unharmed - a fact which caused some to hail Taylor as the living incarnation of his fictional counterpart: "Tommy Taylor made flesh." Some even hailed him as a messiah.

Few, however, would endorse those judgments now, as Taylor prepares to stand trial on six counts of murder. The bloody rampage at the Villa Diodati has silenced most of those voices which previously

NEW

---

http://www.peruugle.com/search/Tommy+Taylor+Switzerla ... ?

Glabutler - 2 hours ago
Journalist and environmentalist George Monbiot said at the so-called End-of-the-World Summit in Patagonia that the time for implementing phased and relatively painless measures to control climate change had come and gone. "It's a question, now, of how hard we hit the wall," he said. "It's difficult not to despair when we see how many last chances have been squandered by ...

AdventAssociation · The ALMANACs

**Librarian Offers to Testify**
LazaroWeekly - 38 minutes ago
Derek Winters, librarian at London's University College, has come forward to talk about his own encounter with Tom Taylor - a scant day before the Villa Diodati murder spree. Winters claims that Tom Taylor came to the College library in search of fictional characters from several Dickens novels, all of whom he claimed to have met. "It was ...

**Policeman in Diodati Case Hospitalized**
ParallelPress - 4 hours ago
A twice-decorated police officer, Louis Pagnol, has been hospitalized for stress after taking part in the murder investigation at the Villa Diodati. Pagnol became increasingly disturbed by the horrendous sights at the Villa, his superior officer, Assistant Commissioner Félis Rousse, has said in a prepared statement: He began to behave aberrantly and to report visual hallucinations. Colleagues removed him from the scene shortly after the arrest of Tom Taylor, during which he claimed to have seen a flying ...

**Is There a Fourteenth Tommy Taylor Novel?**
TeaRooms - 8 hours ago

Speculation mounted yesterday that the renewal by Queensbury Publishing of the copyright protections on existing Tommy Taylor properties, and their extension to territories such as China and Southeast Asia, was a preemptive action designed to prevent pirates and counterfeiters from profiting when a fourteenth Tommy Taylor novel is announced later this year. Editor Ernie Cole refused to respond to questions about whether he has been in contact with missing author Wilson Taylor, and whether Queensbury had received ...

all 2,759 news articles >>

**"Kill with Kindness" Lecturer Dismissed**
PanWNews - 4 hours ago
An academic who suggested that cities and even local communities should be set euthanasia targets in order to cut the global population back to nineteenth century levels has lost his position at the UK's Durham University. Lawrence Ivens claimed that runaway population growth was the biggest threat to the world's future, and insisted that his radical solution posed no ethical challenge. "All societies have culled their populations when they had to," an unrepentant Ivens argued yesterday. "And killing a loved one can actually be an experience that brings you closer ...

AND YOU'RE *TOM TAYLOR.*

YES.

DO YOU EXPECT SPECIAL PRIVILEGES BECAUSE OF WHO YOU ARE?

NO, I--

THERE'S NO CELEBRITY STATUS HERE.

YOU'RE INNOCENT UNTIL PROVEN GUILTY. AND THAT'S THE ONLY DOUBT YOU'LL GET THE BENEFIT OF.

THAT WILL BE ALL FOR NOW.

No celebrity status? For the boy wizard who turned into a screw-up who turned into a mass murderer?

You hear a hollow echo there? Your man inside heard it, loud and clear.

SHOW ME SOME *MAGIC,* PETIT SORCIER.

J'AIME BEAUCOUP ÇA.

SAVOY. TAYLOR. *VOUS ÊTES LÀ-DEDANS.*

GREAT STUFF.

ALL THE COMFORTS OF *HOME.*

GARE DE CORNAVIN. GENEVA.

LIZZIE HEXAM.

ALL RIGHT, I MESSED UP. *PULLMAN* WAS AT THE VILLA.

BY THE TIME I FIGURED OUT WHAT WAS *HAPPENING*, THERE WAS BLOOD AND HAIR ON THE WALLS AND *POLICE* EVERYWHERE. I LOST TOMMY.

*MINGUS* WAS THERE TOO, BUT THEY'VE MANAGED TO KEEP THAT PART OUT OF THE *NEWS*.

RFFFFFFFFFF

Stendhal

Le Rouge et le No...

You got the map. That's the important thing. And you won Tommy's trust. But he's vulnerable now, and they will try to kill him.

YOU THINK I DON'T *KNOW* THAT? BUT THEY'VE TAKEN HIM TO PRISON.

WHATEVER I DO NOW, IT'S GOING TO BE PRETTY *HARD* TO DO IT QUIETLY. YOU SAID YOU DIDN'T WANT ME *SEEN*.

So the inside man asks this: Is Roncevaux prison big enough for Tommy Taylor?

Because you can already see the place starting to creak a little under the strain.

TELL ME A *BEDTIME* STORY, TOMMY.

*T'ES DINGUE?* HE JUST DOES *MURDER* MYSTERIES, THESE DAYS.

THAT SO, TOMMY? YOU GONE ALL *DARK* AND DANGEROUS?

MY NAME'S NOT *TOMMY.*

YEAH, I THINK IT *IS,* MAN.

AND I THINK YOU'RE GONNA TELL ME A--

*NUUUH!*

*PLASTIC* FORK. EVERY ONE OF THESE TINES IS GONNA BREAK OFF IF I STICK IT IN YOUR *EYE,* BUT I THINK IT'LL STILL DO SOME REAL DAMAGE.

WHAT'S MY *NAME?*

T-TOM.

YOUR NAME IS *TOM.*

THANKS, MAN. I **APPRECIATE** IT.

WERE YOU ALWAYS SUCH A *CORIACE?*

A WHAT?

A BAD-ASS. A TOUGH, *MOTHER-FUCKING* SORT OF GENTLEMAN.

NO WAY. I'M A DEVOUT COWARD. THIS IS MORE LIKE--

WHAT?

NOTHING.

I'M STANDING TRIAL FOR *MURDER,* FOR CHRIST'S SAKE.

I GUESS IT'S JUST--YOU KNOW, AFFECTING MY *MIND.*

To be honest, your inside man had had the same thought already.

But he tries never to prejudge.

CLAUDE! T'ES VACHEMENT EN RETARD, HEIN?

I'M SORRY, ADIYA. IT WAS ANOTHER DAY OF **FIRE-FIGHTING.**

THE NEW **WOMEN'S** WING IS TAKING HALF OF MY SQUARE FOOTAGE WITH IT. I MAY EVEN LOSE THE **CHAPEL.**

FORGET ALL THAT NOW. LEON AND COSI ARE STILL **AWAKE.** YOU SHOULD KISS THEM GOODNIGHT.

AND GIVE THEM A **CHAPTER** OR TWO PERHAPS. IT WOULD HELP TO RELAX ME.

I MET TAYLOR HIMSELF TODAY. IT WAS-- A DISPIRITING EXPERIENCE.

IT'S GOING TO BE HARD TO STOP THEM FROM FINDING OUT ABOUT THIS.

HARD OR NOT, IT'S WHAT WE HAVE TO DO. I WON'T HAVE THEIR MINDS POISONED.

HEY THERE, MY LITTLE WIZARDS, YOU'LL TURN INTO **OWLS** IF YOU STAY UP SO LATE.

DADDY!

CAN WE HAVE ANOTHER **CHAPTER?** WE'RE SO CLOSE TO THE END NOW!

WELL, PERHAPS A **PAGE** OR TWO...

Tommy Taylor et la Trompette d'Or

"So," Tommy said, "The Count has sounded the first note on the trumpet. But the world hasn't changed."

"Tommy, I'd like to believe that," Sue replied, anxiously. "But if we've been changed too, we might not even see what's happened to the world."

I WONDER IF THAT COULD **HAPPEN**, DADDY?

IF THE WHOLE WORLD COULD **CHANGE** AND WE WOULDN'T EVEN KNOW!

BUT WE **WOULD** KNOW, COSI.

NOT IF **WE** CHANGED, TOO. IT WOULD BE LIKE HOW ON A **PLANE** YOU'RE MOVING REALLY FAST, AND IT FEELS LIKE YOU'RE STANDING STILL BECAUSE YOU'RE MOVING **WITH** THE PLANE.

I THINK MAYBE THIS BOOK IS TOO **OLD** FOR YOU, LEON.

NO, IT'S **NOT!**

WELL, **MISS BÉNI** IN SCHOOL SAYS TOMMY TAYLOR'S GOT VERY **MATURE** THEMES IN IT.

I'M MATURE. I'M MORE MATURE THAN **YOU!**

ENOUGH, CHILDREN! ENOUGH!

WHAT'S THE FIRST **LESSON** AT TULKINGHORN'S MAGIC CONSERVATORY?

ALL WHO **HAVE** THE SPARK MUST PROTECT AND **STAND** BY THE SPARK!

EXACTLY. YOU'LL GET **EXPELLED** IF YOU PICK FIGHTS WITH EACH OTHER.

"A wizard who perverts his skills, Who cheats or steals or maims or kills, Who charms the last sweet from the packet, Or flees the school when foes attack it, Who scorns his friends or breaks his trust Shall be condemned and come to dust!"

OUI. OUI, LEON.

C'EST BIEN VRAI.

NUUH?

WHAT THE HELL--?

CHAPELLE CATHOLIQUE

LOOK, YOU'RE NOT *REAL*. YOU CAN'T BE.

YOU SAID THE SAME THING TO THE *CAT*.

IT SEEMS A FOOLISH THING TO SAY, IN THE FACE OF SUCH COMPELLING EVIDENCE.

YOU'RE A CHARACTER IN A *BOOK*. A REALLY *OLD* BOOK THAT NOBODY READS.

YOU STANDING THERE--TALKING--IT'S LIKE A BAD JOKE. IF *YOU'RE* REAL, THEN BR'ER RABBIT IS REAL, AND DRACULA. AND THE TOOTH FAIRY.

AND--*CHRIST*, PERHAPS.

YEAH. HIM, TOO.

I UNDERSTAND YOUR *DILEMMA*. IT IS FRIGHTENING TO THINK OF THE WORLD AS HAVING NO FIRM FOUNDATIONS.

FRIGHTENING TO MEET ONE'S *MAKER*.

AND TO FIND HIM... UNSATISFACTORY.

WHAT? WHAT ARE YOU TALKING ABOUT?

YOU. AND MYSELF. WE HAVE THAT IN *COMMON*.

WE ARE *CREATURES*. MADE THINGS. AND THOSE WHO MADE US DO NOT *LOVE* US.

SPEAK FOR YOURSELF.

I SPEAK FOR THOSE WROUGHT AND SHAPED BY MORTAL MEN, FOR *MONSTERS*.

FINE. BUT THAT'S NOT ME.

THEN WHY DID YOU *CALL* ME? AND HOW?

# INSIDE MAN: The Song of Roland

MAGIC ISN'T IN YOUR *REPERTOIRE,* TAYLOR!

IT WAS JUST A JOKE--

IT WAS YOU TRADING ON YOUR *HERITAGE,* YOU ABJECT PIECE OF SCUM!

YOU'RE A--A *REPOSITORY* FOR CHILDREN'S DREAMS! AN ANCHOR POINT IN THEIR IMAGINATIVE *LIVES!*

AND THEN YOU DO THIS MONSTROUS, MONSTROUS THING!

UMM-- INNOCENT UNTIL PROVEN *GUILTY?*

YOU DON'T GET TO *DO* THAT.

YOU DON'T GET TO *USE* THE WORD "INNOCENT."

I LOOK AT YOU AND I SEE WEEPING CHILDREN. *MY* CHILDREN!

*STAINED* AT SECOND HAND BY YOUR FILTHY DEEDS.

TAKE THEM TO THE *ISOLATION* WING. PUT THEM IN SEPARATE CELLS.

YES, SIR.

AND SAY *NOTHING* TO ANYONE ABOUT THIS. I'LL REPORT THE DEATH.

WE HAVE TO *CONTAIN* THIS. KEEP A LID ON SPECULATION.

CONTROL THE WAY THE STORY IS *REPORTED.*

SEARCH: [_____] go

Thursday

# MYSTERIOUS DEATH AT DONOSTIA

Donostia prison, in Southern France, is in the news again today after a guard suffered a fatal fall from an internal walkway. The prison was already under a media spotlight because celebrity murder suspect Tom Taylor is currently being held on remand there, pending trial for the Villa Diodati slayings.

The guard, Martin Busquel, 34, apparently tripped and fell over a safety rail while conducting his ordinary nightly rounds. A press release from prison governor Claude-Louis Chadron emphasized that there are no suspicious circumstances and consequently no need for an external investigation. Local news feeds, however, were reporting before the death was announced that two other guards on the same night shift were admitted to nearby Bois-Terrière Hospital with facial and abdominal injuries.

Donostia seems to have courted controversy many times in recent months. The opening of the new women's wing has unrolled amid accusations from human rights groups that overcrowding at the prison has now reached crisis proportions. The Ministry for the Interior has denied this, stating that Donostia adheres to official guidelines which guarantee every prisoner 30 cubic meters of living space.

Governor Chadron himself has only recently returned from a leave of absence which some allege was to allow him to be treated for work-related stress and depression. If so, he must have wished that Tom Taylor has remained in Switzerland rather than being extradited to

---

## Tommy Taylor Syndrome
by Doctor Pauline Swann

If the health of the human collective unconscious can be measured by our dreams we're in a pretty bad state right now. Six patients in four days have mentioned end-of-the-world dreams in their regular sessions with me. Apocalyptic imagery p angels and trumpets, books with seven seals, great beasts and women clad in the s And one surprise guest star: Tommy Taylor.

There are, I suppose, plenty of very good reasons why people should feel pessimis about the immediate future. The past year has seen the twenty-first century's first pandemic, the near-collapse of the world's economies and the news that the most pessimistic forecasts about global warming were still understating the direness of problem.

But why Tommy Taylor?

The answer to that is a complex one, and it points to the vital importance of story i lives. Ask anyone about *Tommy Taylor and the Cave of Silence*, the first novel in Wils Taylor's modern masterpiece, and they'll instantly be able to tell you where and w they first read it - or when it was read to them, if like me they encountered it first as bedtime story administered in always-too-small doses by indulgent parents.

So Tommy Taylor is emblematic of our childhood: an uncomplicated and sinless pl that was amazingly intense, and spreads its light around the whole of our interior landscape.

Except that the light has been extinguished, or polluted by the lurid red glow of th Diodati murders. It's as though a partner has been unfaithful to us, or we've been estranged from one of our children. The psychic trauma is no less real because it s from an imaginary source. We're all of us sick, and the name of our sickness is Tommy Taylor.

The cure, surely, is to wean ourselves from this dependency. We have to move int post-Tommy state of mental health and resilience - a project that will be difficult, b

---

New
Archive
Find'a'Doc
Be in the book
E-Books
Local Listings
Interviews
Case Studies
FAQ

---

◄ ► ☆ Ω | httq://www.InsideMan.blogtronic.com/PRISONDIARY | Next Blo

😐 [_____] SEARCH BLOG ★

# PRISON DIARY

## INSIDE MAN REPORTS

WEDNESDAY

### Day 1

Z-list celebrity, media whipping boy, suspected savior and now convict.

Tom Taylor's first day at Donostia was a quite memorable one. Whether he's the cold-hearted killer his enemies make him out to be, or the victim of circumstances painted by his few remaining fans, he certainly made an impression here in the arse end of the correctional system, where liberty, equality and fraternity are someone else's problems.

Claude-Louis, our beloved governor, decided to avoid any possible suggestion of favoritism by giving poor Tom the shittiest job in the whole jail - up in the cradle, chipping out old mortar from Donostia's crumbling brickwork so B wing can be repainted and survive another winter.

Eighty feet off the ground, with only Anton "Subway Slayer" Moustaki for company, Tom must have been reflecting on how fleeting fame is, and how fickle the adoration of the sweaty masses. Last week his name was in the prayers of the emotionally retarded of all ages, from Silken Samarkand to Cedared wherever-the-fuck. Today he can't scrape up the change to buy a smoke (one euro or a tenth of a blow-job at Donostia prices).

Night fell, and the cell doors slammed. What did Tom Taylor dream about, as he lay

---

Related Searches: Tommy Taylor, Wilson Taylor, Replica Wands, Golden Trumpet, Tim Hunter, Cosplay Robes, Virginia

All items | Auctions only | *InstaBuy* only | **14,281** results found for **Tom Taylor memorabilia**

Sort by | Best Match

| | Current Price | You Have |
|---|---|---|

**Signed Convention Programme: TommyCon 2006** — *InstaBuy* — $5 — <1m
INSCRIBED "TO SARAH, HOPE THE MAGIC STAYS WITH YOU FOREVER."
OWNER NO LONGER WANTS OR NEEDS

**Death Row Tom. Lmtd edition resin figure set: 136/500** — 62 Bids — $612.00 — 6m
SEND TOM TAYLOR TO THE ELECTRIC CHAIR, GUILLOTINE OR LETHAL CHAMBER: A DIFFERENT EXECUTION EVERY DAY.

**Complete set of Tommy Taylor Novels** — 14 Bids — $178.32 — 7m
ALL 1st EDITIONS EXCEPT FOR Tommy Taylot and the Glass Sword, 3rd PRINTING.
ALL SIGNED BY TOM TAYLOR.

---

**Swordsman55** — Posted: 1:03 am — quote

I don't care what the papers say. Tom is Tommy. He didn't do those things.

Back to top

**SweetSueSparrow** — Posted: 1:10 am — quote

Someone did. If it wasn't him, he really worked hard to make it look like it was.

Back to top

**ZFACTOR** — Posted: 1:12 am — quote

There was meant to be another guy at the villa. Some witnesses said that anyway. I think I read that.

Back to top

**SweetSueSparrow** — Posted: 1:20 am — quote

But the descriptions were all over the place. Someone even said his hand wasn't real, or he had like a wooden glove on or something.

Back to top

**Swordsman55** — Posted: 1:38 pm — quote

Tom is Tommy.

Back to top

**SweetSueSparrow** — Posted: 1:43 pm — quote

Yeah that's the answer to everything Swordsman. Thanks.

Back to top

TV, Movie & Character Toys (456)

Maison d'Arrêt Donostia
Entrée Femmes

ELIZABETH HEXAM.

LOVELY. ONE MORE *MOUTH* TO FEED.

PAPERWORK'S ALL IN THE *BAG*, AND SHE'S QUIET AS A MOUSE. HASN'T SAID A *WORD* SINCE GENEVA.

THEN WE'LL GET ALONG *FINE*.

PERSONAL EFFECTS. PURSE. KEYS. BRACELET. POSTER.

IT'S A *MAP*.

AND I DOORKNOB. SORRY, *FILLETTE*, YOU'LL HAVE TO USE YOUR FINGER LIKE EVERYONE ELSE.

151, INES. TU VAS NOTER CA, HEIN?

ON MANQUE D'ÉTIQUETTES.

TU PARLES. ON MANQUE DE PRESQUE TOUT.

VA, REINETTE. TU PEUX L'EMMENER.

WHAT DO YOU WANT A *MAP* FOR, ANYWAY? IT'LL ONLY REMIND YOU OF WHAT YOU'RE *MISSING*.

WHAT I'M MISSING?

THE *WORLD*, MA BELLE. YOU WON'T BE SEEING IT FOR A WHILE.

DOESN'T MATTER.

I'VE SEEN *BETTER*.

The isolation wing at Donostia isn't as bad as it sounds. Okay, the cell is a box, the cots have no mattress or blankets, and the temperature is a bracing 10 degrees.

But the peace and quiet let a man catch up with his work.

I'M REALLY *SORRY* I GOT YOU INTO THIS, SAVOY.

At least, intermittently.

YOU DIDN'T. I GOT *MYSELF* INTO IT.

I DIDN'T *HAVE* TO FOLLOW YOU, DID I? AND I DIDN'T HAVE TO STEP INTO THAT *PORK ROAST.*

IT'S TOO BAD THE GUY *FELL,* BUT FUCK IT. IF ANYONE'S TO BLAME HERE, IT'S *ME,* FOR NOT KEEPING UP MY PROFESSIONAL STANDARDS.

PROFESSIONAL *STANDARDS?* YOU'RE AN ARMED ROBBER.

TOM, DO YOU BELIEVE *EVERYTHING* YOU'RE TOLD?

THEY BROUGHT ME DOWN FROM *GENEVA* WITH YOU. BUNKED ME IN WITH YOU. EVEN LET ME KEEP MY *PHONE.* YOU DIDN'T THINK THAT WAS STRANGE AT ALL?

I *PAY* FOR ALL THIS. OR AT LEAST, THE COMPANY THAT HOSTS MY *BLOG* DOES.

THE GUARDS POCKET A NICE LITTLE BONUS, AND I GET EXCLUSIVE ACCESS.

I'M A *JOURNALIST,* MAN.

AND YOU'RE THE *STORY.*

I'M TELLING YOU. THREE GUARDS WITH BATONS AND GUNS!

TOM TAYLOR HOSPITALIZED TWO, **KILLED** THE THIRD STONE DEAD.

NO SHIT. I SAW THE **BODY** IN THE HOSPITAL WING.

DOESN'T HAVE TO BE **MAGIC**, ZIZI.

NO, DOESN'T HAVE TO BE. BUT THE DEAD GUY'S **FACE**, YEAH?

IT HAD BEEN RIPPED WIDE OPEN. RIPPED TO THE **BONE**.

AND WHAT ABOUT THE CELL DOOR? HE **OPENED** IT WITHOUT A KEY.

IF HE CAN DO THAT, WHY DIDN'T HE JUST WALK STRAIGHT **OUT**?

BECAUSE HE'S HERE FOR A **REASON**, YOU DUMB BITCH.

HE DIDN'T JUST LET HIMSELF GET ARRESTED BY **ACCIDENT**!

HE CAN ESCAPE WHENEVER HE **WANTS** TO.

HE'S JUST NOT **DONE** HERE YET.

THE SONG WAS LIKE MEDIEVAL *VIRAL MARKETING.* IT SPREAD ACROSS EUROPE, AND STIRRED UP ANTI-MUSLIM FEELING WHEREVER IT WAS *SUNG.*

FRENCH KINGS LED ARMY AFTER ARMY INTO SPAIN TO MAKE IT *CHRISTIAN* AGAIN.

PARTLY BECAUSE THAT SONG KEPT THE OLD *WOUNDS* OPEN AND HURTING.

AT THE *CLIMAX* OF THE STORY, ROLAND--PIERCED WITH A DOZEN WOUNDS--LIFTS UP HIS *HORN,* OLIFANT.

OH YEAH?

*REFUSED* TO DO THIS TWICE--TOO PROUD TO ASK FOR HELP. BUT NOW HE WANTS CHARLEMAGNE TO COME AND *AVENGE* THE DEATHS OF HIS BRAVE KNIGHTS.

HE'S GOT NO *BREATH* LEFT. HE'S BLEEDING OUT, DYING ON HIS KNEES, AND THE *PAGANS* HAVE WON.

THEY'RE MOVING AROUND THE BATTLEFIELD, KILLING THE *WOUNDED,* STRIPPING THE DEAD KNIGHTS' *SADDLE CLOTHS* AS SOUVENIRS.

SO HE USES UP THE LAST OF HIS *STRENGTH.* SUCKS IN A DEEP BREATH--DEEP ENOUGH SO HE CAN FEEL HIS *RIBS* CRACK--

QUOI ENCORE--?

AND HE PUTS THE HORN TO HIS *LIPS.*

TOM!

HE SOUNDS A--

TOM, FOR THE LOVE OF *GOD,* SHUT UP!

WHAT?

SHUT UP AND *LOOK!*

COUNT **TWENTY,** ALL IN!

LOCK UP!

SFLANNG

FLT FLT FLT FLT FLT

MRAOWRRrr

COME ON, YOU LITTLE FLEABAG.

WE'VE GOT WORK TO DO.

"Without a word, the Professor gave Tommy the wand."

"'Until **Glitterspar** is mended,' he said, 'I'd like you to use **Truth.** May she serve you as well as she has me.'"

AND THAT WILL BE ALL FOR TONIGHT, MY LITTLE WIZARDS.

NOT EVEN *ONE* MORE CHAPTER, DADDY?

NON, COSI. I HAVE TO GO BACK TO *WORK*. I HAVE A MEETING.

PROFESSOR TULKINGHORN SHOULD *ADOPT* TOMMY.

HE *LOVES* TOMMY MORE THAN HIS OWN MUM AND DAD DO.

HOW DO YOU *MEASURE* LOVE, LEON?

WITH A LOVE-O-METER?

THAT WOULD BE A VERY USEFUL DEVICE.

BUT I PROMISE YOU, THE LOVE THAT A MOTHER AND FATHER FEEL FOR THEIR CHILDREN--

CLAUDE, THERE'S A PHONE CALL FOR YOU. A MAN NAMED *SKATE*.

HELLO?

GOVERNOR CHADRON. I WAS BEGINNING TO THINK YOU'D *FORGOTTEN* US.

NO. I--I HADN'T FORGOTTEN.

THEN WE'RE *ON*?

YES.

BECAUSE IF YOU'RE STILL AT HOME--

THE GOVERNOR'S HOUSE IS *ADJACENT* TO THE PRISON. I CAN BE THERE IN LESS THAN A MINUTE.

GOOD, EXCELLENT. OFF YOU *GO*, THEN.

NECESSARY EQUIPMENT. DON'T WORRY, YOUR PAYMENT WILL LOOK LIKE A TAX REBATE. NOBODY WILL EVER *CONNECT* YOU WITH WHAT'S ABOUT TO HAPPEN.

I'M NOT *INTERESTED* IN THE MONEY.

BUT NOBODY ELSE IS TO BE HURT. ONLY *TAYLOR.* YOU HAVE TO GIVE ME YOUR WORD.

PLEASE, GOVERNOR CHADRON. I DON'T LIKE TO BE *TOUCHED.*

YOUR *WORD,* MONSIEUR.

OR THIS GOES NO *FURTHER.*

VERY WELL.

MY WORD IS *NOW.*

IF YOU PLEASE.

KLUD

NUUUH!

AS WITH *BIRTH,* SO WITH DEATH.

LET'S MAKE THIS QUICK AND *BLOODY,* GENTLEMEN.

When a book is read, an irrevocable thing happens— a murder, followed by an imposture. The story in the mind murders the story on the page, and takes its place.

"I DON'T WANT TO *DISRUPT* ANY OF YOUR EXISTING SYSTEMS--"

"--BUT THERE ARE CERTAIN NEW *MEASURES* WHICH I INTEND TO IMPLEMENT FROM DAY ONE."

RANDOM SEARCHES OF STAFF LOCKERS? *GOVERNOR CHADRON,* THE MEN ARE USED TO BEING *TRUSTED.*

YES. ALSO, THEY'RE USED TO SELLING CIGARETTES AND *DRUGS* TO INMATES.

THIS WILL NOW *STOP.*

AT THE LAST *INSPECTION,* BEAUNES, DONOSTIA RECEIVED AN APPROVAL RATING OF *THREE.*

THE FLOURISHING *BLACK MARKET*-- THE WILLINGNESS OF GUARDS TO PROVIDE BANNED SUBSTANCES AND CARRY *MESSAGES*--WAS SEEN AS A PARTICULAR AND ENDEMIC PROBLEM.

*ALL* PRISONS HAVE BLACK MARKETS. THEY FUNCTION AS SAFETY VALVES.

*SAFETY* VALVES? BEAUNES, OUR BUSINESS IS *JUSTICE.*

IF WE SET UP UNJUST SYSTEMS, WHAT *MESSAGE* ARE WE SENDING TO THE CONVICTS IN OUR CARE?

GOVERNOR, DON'T TAKE THIS THE WRONG WAY, BUT DO WE WANT TO DO THIS *NOW?*

IF THE *EXTRADITION* COMES THROUGH, AND *TOM TAYLOR* IS SENT HERE, THEN THE EYES OF THE WORLD--

YES, I *KNOW* THE ARGUMENT. DON'T WASH YOUR DIRTY LINEN IN *PUBLIC.*

WHEN WE LOCK A MAN UP, M. BEAUNES, IT'S LIKE LOCKING UP A PART OF OUR OWN HUMAN POTENTIAL. THE *DARK* PART. THE PART WE *FEAR.*

BUT THAT'S WHAT THE LIGHT IS FOR, NO?

TO SHOW THE STAINS.

IT'S GOING TO BE *HARD.* THERE'S A LOT TO DO.

BUT YOU'VE BEEN IN SITUATIONS LIKE THIS *BEFORE,* AND YOU ALWAYS--

*MAXIMUS CONFUSO!!*

IT'S NOT *CONFUSO,* PETER, IT'S *CONFUSIO.* AND YOU HOLD YOUR WAND LIKE THIS.

COSI, ENOUGH.

IT'S OUR *HEXING* LESSON, MUMMY.

YOU KEPT UP THE GAME ALL THROUGH *DINNER.* NOW IT'S QUIET TIME. GO AND DO YOUR *HOMEWORK.*

OH, LEAVE THEM, ADIYA. THERE'S NO *HARM* IN--

MEANWHILE IN SWITZERLAND, THE INQUIRY INTO THE *VILLA DIODATI* SLAYINGS CONTINUES, AS CONTROVERSY GROWS OVER THE FATE OF THE CHIEF *SUSPECT.* THE GOVERNMENT IS CALLING FOR THE EXTRADITION OF--

KLIK

MISS SPARROW. MASTER PRICE. *COUNT AMBROSIO* HAS BEEN SEEN IN THE VICINITY OF THE SCHOOL.

PRAY PROCEED TO YOUR *DORMITORIES* AT ONCE.

YES, PROFESSOR TULKINGHORN!

YOU'RE FUSSING ABOUT **NOTHING**, ADIYA.

ABOUT NOTHING? CLAUDE, SHE'S PAINTING **SPELLS** ON THE WINDOWS.

GUARD SIGILS. SHE'S PLAYING OUT A SCENE FROM THE **BOOK**, THAT'S ALL.

SHE'S **TERRIFIED**. THIS STUFF IS TOO MUCH FOR HER.

NO, IT ISN'T. IT ISN'T AT ALL. THERE'S NOTHING **WRONG** WITH BEING SCARED.

IN THESE BOOKS, GOOD ALWAYS **TRIUMPHS** OVER EVIL. EVIL DEFEATS ITSELF. THERE ARE GOOD LIFE LESSONS TO BE LEARNED HERE.

I WANT HER TO SEE A **PSYCHIATRIST**.

I THINK WE NEED TO **TALK** ABOUT ALL THIS.

ARE WE **SAFE** NOW, SUE?

OF COURSE WE ARE, PETER PRICE.

THIS IS THE **STANDFAST**. THE SIGIL OF IRON AND FIRE.

IT WILL HOLD UNTIL **TOMMY** GETS HERE.

Iran Defies Nuclear Ban...    Toxic Waste Kills 400 Afer Record Spill...    Stem Cell Disaster: Who is Blame...

BIG NEWS: Tom Taylor accomplice...    BW Sues Start-up Publi...    New Tea Discovered in A...    FEED HISTORY

# The POSTnation
### When all else fails, read everything.

# When a Book Becomes a Disease:
## Dr. Pauline Swann and Tommy Taylor

filed by:  Barb. G. Celaeno

Moral Massacre - CBC
Right Rev. Ian Skinner
www.NightlyShow.Nation.com

"The fact is that children come from these books believing that magic is not only *possible* but attractive and desirable.  They *groom* children for Satan!"
- **The Right Rev. Ian Skinner**

Moral Massacre - CBC
Lewis Hale, anthropologist
www.NightlyShow.Nation.com

"Most audiences, for most of human history, haven't *distinguished* between stories and spells. To describe something in words was to summon it, or bind it, or call on its *power*."
- **Lewis Hale**

Watch all your favorite late-night shows at NightlyShow.Nation

**O**n CBC's **Moral Massacre debate show**, broadcast last night at 9.00pm EST, Dr. Pauline Swann astonished the studio audience and her fellow guests by asserting that Tommy Taylor now constitutes a nationwide – perhaps a global – mental health problem.

Dr. Swann, a noted psychotherapist, has already published three books discussing the links between modern culture and mental health.  Now, in *The Poisoned Well*, she turns her theory of cultural bootstrapping on the biggest media target of all: the lovable boy wizard whose exploits have been read by more than a third of humanity.

"Karl Jung suggested that there's a collective human unconscious," Swann said. "An under-mind that feeds all our myths, all our deepest instincts.  That's always been true.  But in an age of mass culture, we can actually write to the under-mind. Our virally spreading fictions embed themselves in the collective unconscious of humanity and change it."

Swann's work remains controversial.  Her most notorious case study – a drawing of Mickey Mouse by a blind autistic child in Peru – has been challenged as a possible fake.

Last night's debate, though, centered on the Tommy Taylor books, and  the extent to which the actions of Tom Taylor, the real-life model for their fictional hero, have "poisoned the well" of children's  imaginations. Reference was made to the blood-bath at the Villa  Diodati, which occurred after the publication of Swann's book but  seems to provide striking support for her thesis.

Watch complete episode at NightlyShow.Nation

Moral Massacre - CBC
Dr. Pauline Swann
www.NightlyShow.Nation.com

"I think there is a pathology, a Tommy Taylor disease.  I've treated children who literally believe they heard the last note of the golden trumpet. Children who are living the apocalypse!"
- **Dr. Swann**

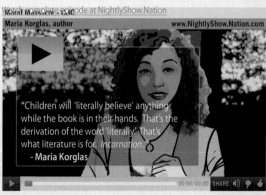

Moral Massacre - CBC
Maria Korglas, author
www.NightlyShow.Nation.com

"Children will 'literally believe' anything while the book is in their hands. That's the derivation of the word 'literally'. That's what literature is for. *Incarnation*."
- **Maria Korglas**

IT'S **TRUE.**

MY **DAD** TOLD ME. AND IT WAS ON THE NEWS.

IT'S **NOT** TRUE.

WHAT DOES IT SAY THERE?

GO ON, WHAT DOES IT **SAY?**

**ABRACADABRA!**
You're Nicked, Tommy!

◄ previous

next ►

**T**om Taylor has been formally charged with the murders at the Villa Diodati. He plans to enter a plea of not guilty, despite what investigating officers are calling a mountain of incriminating evidence, both forensic and circumstan~

IT'S JUST A **STORY.**

NO, **TOMMY TAYLOR** IS JUST A STORY. THIS IS REAL.

HERE'S MY **WAND,** CHADRON: SIT ON IT AND--

OBFUSCUS OCULI!!!

AHHRRRR!

ADIYA--

THE PSYCHIATRIST, CLAUDE. WE CAN'T GO ON LIKE THIS.

CHILDREN HAVE A RIGHT TO DREAM. TO LET THEIR IMAGINATION RUN FREE.

IF THEY CAN'T DO THAT, THEY'RE NOT CHILDREN AT ALL.

SHE ATTACKED TWO OF HER SCHOOLMATES. WE'RE LUCKY ONE OF THEM DIDN'T LOSE AN EYE!

I KNOW. I KNOW.

I'M NOT DISAGREEING WITH YOU. I'M JUST EXPLAINING--

I DON'T NEED EXPLANATIONS. I NEED FOR THIS TO STOP.

I'M GOING TO CALL THAT NUMBER MY SISTER GAVE ME, BACK IN PARIS.

RIGHT, RIGHT. WE'LL SORT THIS.

WE WILL, I PROMISE YOU.

WE'LL SORT THIS AND THEN WE'LL MOVE ON.

AND WHEN YOU PUT THE *GUARD SIGILS* ON YOUR WINDOW, COSI, WHAT ARE THEY MEANT TO KEEP OUT?

*BAD THINGS.*

BAD THINGS LIKE *VAMPIRES?* LIKE COUNT AMBROSIO?

JUST BAD THINGS.

NOBODY'S EVER *SEEN* A VAMPIRE, HAVE THEY?

IT'S HARD TO BELIEVE THEY REALLY *EXIST.*

NOBODY'S EVER SEEN *GERMS,* EITHER. OR THE BIT OF THE *MOON* THAT'S ROUND THE BACK.

MOST PEOPLE HAVEN'T SEEN THE *AMAZON RAIN FOREST.* BUT THEY STILL BELIEVE IT'S THERE.

AND YOU BELIEVE--WHAT? THAT MAGIC *SYMBOLS* CAN KEEP BAD THINGS AWAY?

IT'S JUST A *GAME.*

BUT WHEN YOUR MOTHER WIPED THE SYMBOLS *AWAY,* YOU PUT THEM BACK.

SOMETIMES... EVEN IF IT'S A GAME... IT'S *REAL,* TOO.

SOMETIMES IT'S NOT UP TO YOU TO *CHOOSE.*

YOU DID THIS.

WHAT?

YOU *ENCOURAGE* HER, EVERY TIME. YOU PLAY ALONG. "I AM YOUR BELOVED *HEADMASTER!*"

YOU PUT THIS *GARBAGE* IN HER HEAD, AND NOW IT'S MADE HER SICK.

YOU DON'T UNDERSTAND, ADIYA. YOU DON'T SEE THE *JOY* IN HER EYES WHEN WE-- IT'S SO *IMPORTANT* TO HER.

TO YOU. IT'S IMPORTANT TO *YOU.* AND SHE SEES THAT.

AND NOW THAT TAYLOR BOY IS IN YOUR PRISON, CHARGED WITH TERRIBLE CRIMES.

I'LL *DEAL* WITH THAT.

OF COURSE YOU WILL, CLAUDE. IT'S IN YOUR *JOB* DESCRIPTION.

BUT IT'S NOT IN *HERS.*

SHE'S ONLY IN THIS STATE BECAUSE OF YOU.

I--I THINK PERHAPS I'LL *WALK* BACK. I NEED--

I NEED TO *THINK.*

"YOU'RE A--A *REPOSITORY* FOR CHILDREN'S DREAMS! AN ANCHOR POINT IN THEIR IMAGINATIVE *LIVES!*"

"AND THEN YOU DO THIS MONSTROUS, MONSTROUS THING!"

UMM... INNOCENT UNTIL PROVEN *GUILTY?*

YOU DON'T GET TO *DO* THAT.

YOU DON'T GET TO *USE* THE WORD "INNOCENT."

I LOOK AT YOU AND I SEE WEEPING CHILDREN! *MY* CHILDREN! *STAINED* AT SECOND HAND BY YOUR FILTHY DEEDS.

TAKE THEM TO THE *ISOLATION* WING.

PUT THEM IN SEPARATE CELLS.

GOVERNOR--

--SHOULD I INVESTIGATE TAYLOR'S *ALLEGATIONS* FURTHER?

WHY WOULD THAT BE NECESSARY?

WELL, GIVEN WHAT YOU'VE SAID ABOUT *CORRUPTION.* IF THE GUARDS WERE *BRIBED* TO--

THE GUARDS ARE MEN OF GOOD CHARACTER, MEN WITH *FAMILIES.*

TAYLOR'S WORD COUNTS FOR *NOTHING* AGAINST THEIRS.

COSI...?

IS EVERYTHING OKAY?

YES.

DO YOU WANT A SOUR TWIST?

NO.

IS IT TIME FOR OUR HEXING LESSON?

I CAN'T BE *SUE* TODAY, LEON. IF I'M SUE, MUM WILL *SHOUT* AT DAD AND THEN SHE'LL CRY.

OH. OKAY.

BUT-- --I CAN STILL BE *PETER*, CAN'T I?

...

REFRESH THE *WARDS* ON ALL THE DOORS AND WINDOWS.

ON IT!

AND DO A *BENEFICUS* CHARM! IT'S IN TOMMY TAYLOR AND THE UNDEAD KING!

QUICK, BEFORE DAD COMES UP TO READ US OUR *STORY!*

AND THAT WILL BE ALL FOR *TONIGHT,* MY LITTLE WIZARDS.

Tommy Taylor et la Trompette Dorée

NOT EVEN *ONE* MORE CHAPTER, DADDY?

NO, COSI. I HAVE TO GO BACK TO *WORK.*

I HAVE A MEETING.

PROFESSOR TULKINGHORN SHOULD *ADOPT* TOMMY.

HE *LOVES* TOMMY MORE THAN HIS OWN MAMA AND PAPA DO.

HOW DO YOU *MEASURE* LOVE, LEON?

WITH A LOVE-O-METER?

THAT WOULD BE A VERY *USEFUL* DEVICE.

BUT I PROMISE YOU, THE LOVE THAT A MOTHER AND FATHER FEEL FOR THEIR CHILDREN--

CLAUDE--

--THERE'S A PHONE CALL FOR YOU--

--A MAN NAMED *SKATE.*

YOU DID IT *AGAIN.*

YES. ONE LAST TIME, ADIYA.

CLAUDE, I THOUGHT WE *AGREED*--

ONE LAST TIME.

THE REST OF MY LIFE IS *DROWNING* IN FILTH AND COMPROMISE. THIS *OASIS,* THIS PLACE OF PERFECT INNOCENCE-- IT WAS PRECIOUS TO ME.

AFTER TONIGHT--NO MORE. NO MORE *WORRIES* ON THIS. I PROMISE.

HELLO?

GOVERNOR CHADRON. I WAS BEGINNING TO THINK YOU'D *FORGOTTEN* US.

LEON?

ARE YOU AWAKE?

YES. I'M *SCARED,* COSI.

SO AM I.

DAD SAID HE'S GOT *TOMMY* IN HIS PRISON!

IT'S A *TRAP* SET BY COUNT AMBROSIO.

HE'S WORKING ON A NEW *PLAN,* AND HE DOESN'T WANT TOMMY TO BE ABLE TO STOP HIM.

BUT WHAT ABOUT DAD? IS HE *WORKING* FOR COUNT AMBROSIO?

IT'S THE *SOMNAMBULUS* CHARM.

DAD IS IN THE COUNT'S POWER.

HE CAN'T *HELP* HIMSELF.

COSI--

--WHY IS IT SO *BRIGHT* IN HERE?

GET DRESSED.

WHAT?

FIND YOUR TORCH. AND YOUR *WAND*. IT'S UP TO *US*, PETER PRICE.

IF YOU'RE *BRAVE* ENOUGH.

WE'RE GOING TO *RESCUE* TOMMY.

So there's this whole thing in the Tommy Taylor novels about good and evil, okay?

And if I've got it right, it works like this:

Count Ambrosio is immortal because he's an embodiment of something in the human soul.

An inner voice that never stops screaming.

A remorseless, selfish part of ourselves.

He's the bit of us that follows its own logic to the last degree.

As though conscience and grace never existed.

And I buy that, as far as it goes. I think evil is immortal.

I just think the reason is more banal than that.

CLACK

HADRON
19-4613

NOW!!

Your man inside believes this: most guys just take the money and do the job.

Whatever the job happens to be.

RUCKARUCKARUCKARUCKARUCK

# INSIDE MAN CONCLUSION

ENOUGH.

LOOK AT THEIR FACES. *NEITHER* OF THESE MEN IS TAYLOR.

THEY MUST HAVE *MOVED* HIM.

EVIDENTLY. CHECK THE SICK BAY, THE SOLITARY WING, THE COMMON SPACES.

FIND HIM. *FINISH* THIS. AS LOUDLY AND AS *MESSILY* AS POSSIBLE.

WHAT IS IT? WHO IS IT FROM?

IT'S FROM A *FRIEND*.

A FRIEND WHO USES *FLYING CAT MAIL*? COME ON, TAYLOR, TELL ME WHAT IT SAYS!

THE PEOPLE WHO TRIED TO *KILL* ME--SHE SAYS THEY'RE HERE. NOW.

SHE SAYS THEY'RE GOING TO TRY *AGAIN*.

YOU--YOU THINK IT'S *TRUE*?

I DON'T KNOW. IF IT'S TRUE, THEN WE'RE *SCREWED*.

LIZZIE'S GOT A *PLAN*, BUT I HAVE TO GET OUT OF THIS CELL TO MAKE IT WORK.

OH YEAH?

THEN MAYBE THIS WOULD BE A GOOD TIME TO SAY: "DOORS-IUS, SPLAY LIKE A TEN DOLLAR WHORE-IUS."

TIMER 00:00

SFLANNNG

HOW IN *HELL* DID YOU--?

IT'S A *FIRE ALARM*, TAYLOR. DOORS OPEN THREE MINUTES AFTER IT SOUNDS, UNLESS SOMEONE HITS THE *SHUT-OFF*.

TOO MANY TOASTED *INMATES* WHEN THE SCHIPOL JAIL WENT UP.

D-DADDY!

COSI! LEON! WHAT IN GOD'S NAME ARE YOU *DOING* HERE?

WE CAME TO *SAVE* TOMMY!

*YOU!*

GOVERNOR WHATEVER-YOUR-NAME-IS. LISTEN, I JUST NEED THAT THING THE LITTLE GIRL IS *CARRYING.*

IF YOU GIVE IT TO ME, I CAN GET US ALL--

THEY WERE MEANT TO *KILL* YOU!

WHY ARE YOU STILL *ALIVE?* *WHY?*

DADDY! STOP! THIS IS ALL *YOUR* FAULT!

*WAKE UP!*

YOU LET AMBROSIO *SOMNAMBULUS* YOU!

YOU TURNED INTO A MONSTER AND LOCKED UP TOMMY SOMEWHERE IN YOUR PRISON!

NO! COSI, NO, YOU DON'T UNDERSTAND. I DID THIS FOR *YOU.* I--

THERE NOW. I SEE YOU.

AROOOOOOOOOOOOO

HE GOT *AWAY.*

DON'T *ASK.* JUST SPREAD OUT AND COVER THE GATES.

IF YOU SEE HIM, SQUEEZE OFF A *SHOT.* AS MANY SHOTS AS YOU CAN.

STILL *ALIVE,* GOVERNOR CHADRON?

WE'VE GOT TO RUN, AND WE'VE LEFT A LITTLE *MESS* YOU MAY NEED TO--

...

I HAVE COME *FAR,* AND I AM WEARY.

*GUUUH!*

I NEED *SUSTENANCE.*

BLAM BLAM BLAM

HOLY CHRIST!

ARE WE *DEAD* OR SOMETHING? BECAUSE THIS LOOKS LIKE--

TOMMY, YOU GOT IT *WRONG*. TRY AGAIN.

TRY AGAIN. *QUICKLY.*

ONTO IT. ONE MAGIC DOORKNOB, COMING RIGHT--

WHAT THE HELL?

THIS--THIS MUST BE SOME KIND OF *HOLOGRAM.*

HOY! WAS *MACHST* DU DORT?

DU KANNST DICH NICHT HIER *BUMMELN*--AUF DER ANDEREN SEITE! SOFORT!

OH, SHIT! THOSE ARE STORMTROOPERS. *STORMTROOPERS* ARE LOOKING OUR WAY!

UMM, WIR SIND-- NOT FROM *AROUND* HERE, AND--

WE WERE JUST *LEAVING*. MACH SCHNELL. AS SOON AS WE--

HAH!

ERREICHT DIESES *FAHRRAD* AUS HIER HERAUS!

ENTSHULDIGEN, OFFIZIER.

ES TUT MIR LIED.

...LIKE *GHOSTS* OR SOMETHING. THIS IS FUCKING INSANE!

I THINK THIS MUST BE *STUTTGART.*

YEAH, BUT SWASTIKAS? STORMTROOPERS?

IT'S STUTTGART IN *1940.*

WHAT THE FUCK? HEY! HEXAM!

YOU CAN'T *SAY* THAT AND THEN WALK AWAY!

I JUST NEED TO GET MY *BEARINGS.* I'LL BE BACK.

SHIT. THE GHOST OF THE FUCKING SECOND WORLD *WAR?* I'M SUPPOSED TO JUST *SWALLOW* THAT?

SAVOY, GIVE ME YOUR MATCHES.

WHAT?

YOUR *MATCHES.*

THIS *BULLSHIT* ENDS NOW.

AN DIE STELLE DIESES HOFFENS HABEN WIR NUN EIN ANDERED HOFFEN GESETZT, NÄMLICH DAS HOFFEN AUF DIE EINZIGE HILFE, DIE ES EN DIESER WELT GIBT, DIE HILFE DURCH DIE EIGENE KRAFT.

LIZZIE.

WHAT DO YOU WANT FROM ME, TOM?

WHAT DO I WANT?

TAKE A WILD *GUESS.*

WHEREVER I GO, PEOPLE ARE *DYING.* AT THE VILLA. AT DONOSTIA. I'M LIKE A FUCKING *PLAGUE.*

I JUST SAW TWO *KIDS* GET KILLED-- RIPPED TO PIECES--BECAUSE OF ME. AND I COULDN'T DO A BLIND THING TO *STOP* IT.

IT WASN'T YOUR *FAULT.*

I DON'T CARE, LIZZIE. I REALLY *DON'T.*

I NEED TO KNOW WHAT'S *HAPPEN-ING* TO ME.

WHAT *GAME* THIS IS WHERE EVERY-ONE KNOWS THE RULES EXCEPT ME.

AND YOU? YOU'VE BEEN *SHADOWING* ME EVER SINCE LONDON. EVER SINCE TOMMYCON.

THROWING ME INTO THIS SHIT AND THEN DRAGGING ME *OUT* AGAIN. WHY? WHAT THE FUCK DOES IT MEAN?

LOOK AT THE *MAP.*

THE MAP?

YES.

WHY?

BECAUSE THAT'S WHY WE'RE *HERE*, TOMMY.

YOU SEE?

I DON'T SEE *ANYTHING.* MOST OF THESE COASTLINES DON'T EVEN LOOK LIKE--

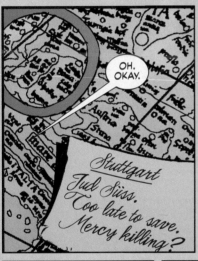

OH. OKAY.

Stuttgart
Jud Süss.
Too late to save.
Mercy killing?

SO *STUTTGART'S* ON THERE. AND THERE'S A NOTE.

*"JUD SÜSS? TOO LATE TO SAVE?"* I DON'T GET IT.

I CAN'T *EXPLAIN* JUST YET, TOMMY.

PLEASE BELIEVE ME. I CAN'T.

WELL, THAT'S A REAL *PITY.*

BECAUSE IN THAT CASE--

--I'M ABOUT TO MAKE A *BONFIRE* OUT OF WHAT YOU CALLED "MY DESTINY."

TSHRIFFF

NO! TOMMY, YOU *CAN'T*! PLEASE!

WHY NOT? WHAT AM *I* GETTING OUT OF ALL THIS?

MY LIFE IS IN RUINS! TWO KIDS ARE *DEAD*, AND WHY? THE SHOW MUST GO ON?

IT WILL ALL MAKE SENSE. YOU--YOU WALK THE *PATH*, AND THEN--

AT THE END, THE *BLESSING* COMES.

YOU'LL UNDERSTAND, THEN. BUT IF I SAY IT, IT WON'T HAPPEN!

TOO BAD.

THERE SHE *GOES*.

NO! YOU MUSTN'T!

YOU *MUSTN'T*!

THEN *TALK* TO ME!

PLEASE--

TALK, OR I'LL JUST STRIKE *ANOTHER* MATCH!

YOUR *FATHER*!!

WH-WHAT?

DON'T YOU UNDERSTAND? THIS IS WHAT HE **WANTED** FOR YOU!

WHAT HE **MADE** YOU FOR!

WHAT ARE YOU TALKING ABOUT?

HOW DO **YOU** KNOW MY FATHER?

HE SET ME FREE. HE MADE ME **REAL.** THE SAME WAY HE DID YOU.

AND WE'RE **NOTHING** WITHOUT HIM. LESS THAN NOTHING.

WE DO HIS WILL BECAUSE THAT'S WHAT WE'RE **FOR,** TOMMY.

THAT'S **ALL** WE'RE FOR!

LIZZIE!

MAP'S OKAY.

THANKS, SAVOY.

PLEASURE, TOTALLY.

SO, UM--

--YOU GOT ANY MAGIC THAT MIGHT ACTUALLY **WORK?**

DONOSTIA JAIL.

07:52 AM.

YOU GET ANYTHING OUT OF THE *MOTHER* YET?

NOTHING WE CAN USE. SHE IDENTIFIED THE *BODIES,* THEN WENT INTO HYSTERICS.

THEY HAD TO *SEDATE* HER.

WHAT THE FUCK WERE TWO KIDS *DOING* HERE IN THE FIRST PLACE?

NOT ONE STINKING *PIECE* OF THIS MAKES ANY SENSE.

AND *TAYLOR?*

MISSING.

ALONG WITH SAVOY, MOUSTAKI, AND MAYBE SOMEONE FROM THE *WOMEN'S* WING. WE'RE STILL RUNNING NAMES.

WHERE YOU GOING?

TO GET SOME *STATEMENTS.*

FROM HARDENED *CONS?* GOOD LUCK.

SOMETIMES THEY RELAX THE *OMERTA* STUFF WHEN A KID GETS CROAKED. IT'S WORTH A TRY.

I MEAN, AT LEAST IT LOOKS LIKE WE'RE DOING *SOMETHING,* RIGHT?

¦UFFF!¦

WHO THE FUCK ARE-- -HKKKK!-

You will speak when I **address** you, son of Adam.

And not until.

Where is **Tommy**?

YOU--YOU MEAN TAYLOR? WE HAVEN'T **FOUND** HIM YET. WE THINK HE **DIED** IN THE FIRE.

Tommy? Dead? No, I would have **felt** it.

He's escaped me, and now I'll have to hunt him down again. For **that**, I'll need both eyes and ears.

May I borrow **yours**?

S-SURE. COME ON DOWN TO THE **PRECINCT**, AND WE'LL--

--WE'LL SEE WHAT WE CAN DO.

Thank you.

But why **wait**?

NICE NIGHT FOR A BOOK-BURNING. I THINK SHE CAME THIS WAY.

HOW DO YOU *KNOW* THAT, SAVOY? SHE COULD BE ANYWHERE.

YEAH, BUT "ANYWHERE" ISN'T ALL THAT *BIG*.

YOU TAKE THE WRONG TURNING, ALL THE *DETAIL* STARTS TO BLEACH OUT.

IT'S LIKE WE'RE IN ONE OF THOSE *MAZES* WHERE ALL THE PATHS LEAD IN TOWARDS THE CENTER.

THERE'S ONLY *ONE* WAY TO GO.

SO THAT WAS SOME CRAZY FUCKED-UP SHIT WITH YOUR *DAD*, HUH? SICCING THE SCARY CHICK ON YOU.

I DON'T WANT TO *TALK* ABOUT IT.

GOD, NO. I DON'T BLAME YOU. BUT IF YOU EVER DO, TALK TO *ME*, RIGHT? I'M SYNDICATED.

DROP DEAD, SAVOY. EVERYWHERE I GO, YOU JOURNALISTS ARE ON ME LIKE FUCKING *VULTURES*.

HEY, THAT WAS SELF-EFFACING HUMOR.

WAIT!

THAT *MAN*--I'VE SEEN HIM BEFORE. HIS NAME'S *PULLMAN*.

AND YOU KNOW HIM HOW?

YOU CAN *SEE* US.

NATÜRLICH. WHY IS THIS *SURPRISING* TO YOU?

BECAUSE NOBODY *ELSE* CAN.

INTERESTING. PERHAPS I AM *DIFFERENT* FROM THOSE OTHERS.

HAVE YOU *CONSIDERED* THIS?

HE LOOKS A LITTLE MORE *REAL*, SOMEHOW.

YEAH, BUT HE *DIDN'T* WHEN WE FIRST CAME IN. IS THIS SOMETHING *WE* DID TO YOU?

JA, *RICHTIG.* JUST SO.

I SENSE THIS. DESPITE APPEARANCES, I AM-- NOT *MYSELF.* WHATEVER IS HAPPENING HERE, IT ORIGINATES WITH *YOU.*

YOU ARE *SOLID* MEN, WALKING AMONG MEN OF SMOKE AND SHADOW.

YOU'RE GHOSTS?

*GESPENSTER? NEIN.* ECHOES. WE ARE *ECHOES,* RAISED BY YOUR PROXIMITY.

AND BY YOUR *ATTENTION,* YES?

COMPARED TO ME, EVEN YOUR *GAZE* IS A SOLID THING. WHEN IT *FOCUSES* ON ME, I BECOME MORE REAL.

FUNNY. A LOT OF PEOPLE HAVE BEEN TELLING ME I'M *LESS* REAL THAN EVERYONE ELSE. THAT I'M A CHARACTER FROM A *BOOK.*

NOW *YOU'RE* TELLING ME THE EXACT OPPOSITE.

A *FICTIONAL* CHARACTER? *HA!*

THAT'S *FUNNY* TO YOU?

YES, IT'S FUNNY. FIGMENTS AND FANTASIES ARE MY AREA OF *EXPERTISE.*

I ASSURE YOU, YOU ARE *NEITHER.*

NO. IF ANYTHING, YOU ARE *TOO* SOLID. INVESTED WITH TOO MUCH *REALITY.* FASCINATING.

IF YOU HAD ARRIVED *EARLIER,* I WOULD HAVE LOVED TO SHOW YOU TO--BUT NO MATTER.

TO *PULLMAN,* YOU MEAN?

YOU *KNOW* HIM? I AM SURPRISED. HE IS A *SERVANT* OF MINE.

A *MESSENGER,* RATHER--BETWEEN MYSELF AND SOME FRIENDS WITH WHOM I SHARE A COMMON *INTEREST.*

I DON'T LIKE *ANY* OF THIS, TAYLOR. LET'S GET THE FUCK OUT OF HERE.

A COMMON INTEREST IN *WHAT?*

IN *LIES.* AND IN THE TRUTHS WHICH ARE THEIR OPPOSITES.

PERMIT ME, PLEASE, A SMALL *ILLUSTRATION.*

IT'S ONE THAT'S VERY *CLOSE* TO MY HEART.

NEIN! NEIN! LASSEN SIE MICH IN *RUHE!*

ENTSCHULDIGEN, SCHATZLEIN. ICH WILLE NICHT.

DIEN *JUNGFRAÜLICHKEIT* FÜR DEINE MANNES LEBEN!

"NO! NO! LEAVE ME BE!"

"PARDON ME, MY DEAR, BUT I WILL NOT."

"YOUR *VIRTUE* FOR YOUR HUSBAND'S LIFE!"

"YOUR *VIRTUE* FOR YOUR HUSBAND'S LIFE." THE *JEW,* YOU SEE, RESPECTS NOTHING.

THE LAW, THE MARRIAGE BOND, LOVE OF *COUNTRY* OR OF HONOR.

DO YOU *BELIEVE* THAT SHIT? OR DO YOU JUST PEDDLE IT?

"I BELIEVE THAT *OTHERS* SHOULD BELIEVE IT.

"BELIEFS ARE *COLLARS* TO WHICH LEASHES CAN BE ATTACHED."

STUTTGART. BUT NOT THE *REAL* STUTTGART? I DON'T LIKE THE SOUND OF THIS AT ALL.

*SWASTIKAS.* NAZI INSIGNIA. STORMTROOPERS.

IT'S JUD SÜSS, THEN.

I THINK SO.

TELL ME WHAT YOU'RE *SEEING.*

YOU HAVE TO TELL TOMMY TO *IGNORE* IT. HE'S NOT STRONG ENOUGH YET.

TOMMY'S NOT *HERE.*

WHAT?

I-- I RAN AWAY. WE *ARGUED,* AND I--

DON'T *TELL* ME ABOUT IT, YOU STUPID CHILD. THERE'S NO TIME TO BE LOST.

I'M SORRY. I'M SORRY, WILSON.

FIND HIM. WARN HIM ABOUT THE *FOCUS* EFFECT.

IDEALLY BEFORE HE *EXPERIENCES* IT FOR HIM-SELF.

# Jud Süss
## The Canker

MY GOD, YOU JUST *MURDERED* HIM. WAS IT BECAUSE HE FIGURED YOU OUT?

EXCUSE ME?

HE KNEW YOU WERE LIKE US. SOMEONE FROM THE *REAL* WORLD.

I AM WHO I *SAID* I WAS. YOU ARE MERELY VERY *SLOW* IN YOUR UNDERSTANDING.

I TOLD YOU THAT YOUR *ATTENTION* WOULD MAKE ME MORE SOLID. YET YOU *CONTINUED* TO ATTEND TO ME.

SHIT! YOU MEAN--

YOU GAVE ME WEIGHT AND MASS. MY *GUN,* AND THE BULLETS WITHIN IT, WERE SWEPT UP IN THE SAME PROCESS.

A *CHILD* WOULD HAVE REALIZED THIS.

SO THIS IS THE OBJECT, JA? WHAT DOES IT *DO?*

IT OPENS *DOORS.*

EXPLAIN.

I CAN'T.

THEN *SHOW* ME.

IT DOESN'T *WORK* HERE.

IF IT DID, WE'D BE *GONE* ALREADY. AND THIS SHIT-STORM WOULDN'T HAVE COME DOWN ON US.

YOU THINK I AM A **FOOL?** YOU WOULD NOT HAVE COME HERE IF YOU DID NOT KNOW HOW TO **LEAVE** AGAIN.

WE WEREN'T **TRYING** TO COME HERE! WE WERE ON OUR WAY TO SOME-PLACE ELSE!

SO, YOU DO NOT KNOW THE USE OF THESE THINGS.

YOU **STOLE** THEM, YES? TELL ME THE NAME OF THEIR TRUE OWNER.

THEY BELONG TO **HIM,** YOU NAZI FUCKWIT. THE GUY ON THE FLOOR.

THAT'S SORT OF THE **PROBLEM** WITH SHOOTING FIRST AND ASKING QUESTIONS LATER.

I SEE. THEN THERE'S NOTHING TO BE **GAINED** BY KEEP-ING YOU ALIVE.

**WAIT! WAIT!**

FOR WHAT? ANYTHING YOU SAY NOW WILL BE A **LIE.**

THE--THE **MOVIE** PROJECTOR.

YES. WHAT ABOUT IT?

WHEN YOU WERE SHOWING US THE MOVIE-- **JUD SÜSS--** I GUESS--

--I GUESS WE FOCUSED OUR ATTENTION ON THE **PROJECTOR,** TOO.

"Some treasure house!" Peter exclaimed. "There's no treasure here." His voice reverberated in the cavernous, empty space.

Tommy frowned, looking back towards the door through which they had entered. The doorknob glittered with a faint, silvery sheen.

"Perhaps we're just not looking in the right place," Tommy murmured.

JESUS!

OW!

¡UFFF!

THIS *ISN'T* THE VILLA DIODATI.

NO. IT LOOKS MORE LIKE *LONDON.* BUT WHAT THE *FUCK.* WE'RE OUT OF THAT *SHIT-HOLE,* ANYWAY. THAT'S WHAT *COUNTS.*

LIZZIE, THIS THING--WHAT WILSON IS DOING--IT'S A LOT *BIGGER* THAN ME, ISN'T IT?

WHAT DO YOU MEAN?

I MEAN IT GOES BACK BEFORE I WAS *BORN.* PEOPLE HAVE BEEN DYING FOR IT, *KILLING* FOR IT, SINCE THE SECOND WORLD WAR.

OH SHIT! LOOK AT THE DATE...

WE'RE OFFICIALLY *OLD* NEWS. WE WERE IN THERE FOR *THREE MONTHS.*

I'M THREE MONTHS PAST MY FUCKING *DEADLINE!*

THE POST

[N]EW TOMMY TAYLOR [T]O SHATTER RECORD[S]

Will Wilson Taylor reappear

UK-based Queensberry Publish[...] are bracing themselves for the biggest book launch the world has ever seen. Millions of fans all over the world have responded with delight to the news that their favorite fictional [...] [a]nd that questions as to his fate will finally be answered after [...] hiatus of more than ten [...] Speculation as to [...] [...]ing mess[...]

NO, THAT'S GOOD. IT MEANS THEY'LL HAVE STOPPED *LOOKING* FOR US.

I'VE GOT TO FIND MY DAD. FIND OUT WHAT'S REALLY GOING ON. WHO *PULLMAN* AND HIS FRIENDS ARE, AND WHAT THEY WANT.

But the sparrows who live at the edge of the wood happened to see.

NUUUH!

They caught Mr. Bun by his ears and his tail.

They flew him high into the air.

NO! FUCKING NO!

TAKE ME TO THE BOTTOM! I WANT OUT OF THIS SHIT-HOLE!

Just imagine how surprised the other animals were to see a flying rabbit!

And they let him down at last, most gently and carefully, back in the heart of the wood--

NO.

NO.

NO.

--just in time for tea.

YEAAARGHHHH!

# Eliza Mae Hertford's Willowbank Tales

Mr. Bun was *screaming* again, Nedward.

So we brought him to *see* you.

Thank you, Tig Hedgehog. Put him over there by my *thistle* patch.

And we'll have a little *talk.*

FUCK FUCK FUCK FUCK FUCK FUCK FUCK

Oh dear, Mr. Bun. Are you in another one of your grumpy moods?

*UNTIE* ME AND FIND OUT, YOU HAIRLESS FUCKING RETARD.

This just won't *do,* you know.

You have so many friends in Willowbank Wood. Tig, and Dogling, and Wilfred Weasel, and Mrs. Matilda Mouse.

Why do you keep trying to *leave* us, when we love you so much?

BECAUSE YOU'RE ANIMALS. AND YOU'RE NOT EVEN *REAL* ANIMALS.

IF YOU WERE REAL, WILFRED WEASEL WOULD *EAT* MRS. FUCKING MATILDA MOUSE WITHOUT EVEN SPITTING OUT THE *BONES.*

Oh, Mr. Bun, the *stories* you tell!

I DON'T *TELL* THEM, YOU FLEA-BITTEN FUCK--I JUST *LIVE* IN THEM.

YOU LET *WILSON TAYLOR* CATCH YOU WITH YOUR GUARD DOWN, AND THIS IS WHERE YOU END UP.

I THOUGHT THE VILLA WAS *EMPTY.* HE WASN'T SUPPOSED TO BE THERE.

I HAD THE MAP RIGHT IN MY FUCKING *HANDS.*

THE NEXT THING I KNOW, HE'S BEATING SEVEN KINDS OF *SHIT* OUT OF ME. AND THEN--

--THEN I WAKE UP *HERE!*

HAH!

Mr. Bun seems a little *calmer* now, Tig.

Yes, Nedward.

I think you should take him back to his *burrow* and let him rest for a while.

PAULY BRUCKNER!

PAULY BRUCKNER!

*PAULY BRUUUUUUUCK-NERRRR!*

I'm leaving a nice *carrot* here, Mr. Bun.

You can *eat* it when you're feeling better.

Why is Mr. Bun *unhappy,* Tig?

Because he's so *clever,* Dogling. Thinking makes your *brain* hurt.

Have *you* ever tried it?

I *have* no brain, Dogling.

Oh.

It was quite usual for Mr. Bun to sulk in his hole for a day or more, after one of his little adventures went wrong.

The other animals stayed away at these times, until he became his old self again.

But this time was worse than the other times. Mr. Bun felt like a clock that has been over-wound.

And he didn't seem able to unwind himself again, no matter how hard he tried.

So finally he went to see Nutshell.

Because Nutshell had something that he needed.

HEY. YOU. CUNT-WHISKER.

GET **DOWN** HERE.

**NOW.**

*AAAA!*

I'm good. I'm good I'm good I'm good.

Get thee *behind* me, rabbit.

IF I DO, IT WILL BE TO REAM YOU OUT WITH A BROKEN **BRANCH,** YOU FUCKING LITTLE COWARD.

I've been washed clean of *sin.* I'm with Christ, now.

For all who enter the kingdom of **heaven** must come there as children. And he suffers the little children to--

*Ufff!*

YOU'VE GONE *NATIVE.* YOU'RE NOT EVEN *TRYING* TO FIGHT THIS.

YOU FUCKING *DISGUST* ME, NIELSON!

THEN LEAVE ME *ALONE,* PAULY.

I--I DON'T EVER *THINK* ABOUT THOSE DAYS, EXCEPT WHEN I SEE *YOU.* PLEASE, JUST LEAVE ME ALONE.

I'D LOVE TO. BUT YOU READ THE *BOOKS,* DIDN'T YOU? TALES OF THE WILLOWBANK WOOD, BY ELIZA MAE HERTFORD.

I--YEAH, I KNOW THEM. I HAD THE WHOLE *SET.* FIRST EDITIONS.

EXACTLY.

SO TELL ME ABOUT THE *HOUSE.*

THE HOUSE? *ROSE TREE COTTAGE?* THAT WAS WHERE ELIZA MAE HERTFORD LIVED AS A KID.

IN THE BOOKS, *"MISS LIZA"* LIVES THERE. BUT THE ANIMALS DON'T GET TO *SEE* HER ALL THAT MUCH.

AND WHERE DO I *FIND* IT?

THERE'S-- UHH!--THERE'S A *PATH.*

FROM THE BIG OAK, OVER THE MILL RACE *BRIDGE,* TO THE COTTAGE.

PAULY, YOU SHOULD JUST *FORGET* IT.

I'M GOING TO FINISH THE JOB. GET THE MAP. FIND THE *MAANIM,* AND BLOW IT THE FUCK UP.

DO UNTO OTHERS, NIELSON. CHECK IT OUT.

IT'S IN THE *BIBLE.*

Now that his work was done, Mr. Bun went to find his friends ~~So-Called.~~ Tig and Dogling.

SO-CALLED.

YOU TWO. I **NEED** YOU.

Really, Mr. Bun?

YOU THINK I'D LIE ABOUT SOMETHING THAT **DEMEANING?** ON YOUR FEET.

We'll have to finish our game of *throw-the-stick* later, Dogling.

Yes. Remember that you were *winning*, Tig.

If I forget, I hope you'll *remind* me.

Where are we going, Mr. Bun?

ROSE TREE COTTAGE.

I FIGURE I'VE GOT A BETTER CHANCE OF **GETTING** THERE IF I'VE GOT TWO ACTUAL **CHARACTERS** WITH ME.

AND THEN WE'LL SEE WHAT WE'LL **SEE**, WON'T WE?

OH, YES.

It's just the time of day when a little *something* might go down very nicely.

My, look how high the *sun* is.

I wonder if it might be time for a *snack.*

At this point in the afternoon, I often stop for a--

DO YOU WANT ME TO PICK UP THAT ROCK AND BEAT YOUR *SKULL* TWO-DIMENSIONAL?

No.

THEN SHUT THE FUCK UP.

FOSTER'S MEADOW

ROSE TREE COTTAGE

WILLOWBANK WOOD

FARTHEST FOREST

OKAY, THIS IS GOOD. THIS IS *VERY* GOOD.

YOU TWO CAN GET *LOST* NOW. I DON'T NEED YOU ANY MORE.

But we're your friends.

MY *FRIENDS* HAVE OPPOSABLE THUMBS.

And perhaps after the *adventure,* we can have a picnic.

JESUS FUCKING *WEPT.*

BINGO. X MARKS THE SPOT. BUT WHY IS THE *GATE* WIDE OPEN?

I THOUGHT THIS WAS A "FARMER McGREGOR'S GARDEN" KIND OF DEAL.

There *is* a garden. Miss Liza lets all the animals help themselves to the *vegetables*.

If they happen to be hungry...

But we can't go into the *house*, because she might be doing her homework.

And she can't come out and *play* until it's done.

NO SHIT.

Where are we going, Mr. Bun?

TO THE *HOUSE*.

But we just told you--

I'M THE KIND OF RABBIT WHO CAN'T BE *TOLD*.

THERE! HOLD IT THERE!

It's-- it's too *heavy!*

JUST A SECOND LONGER--

*Nuuuh!*

*AAAHRRR!*

M-Mr. Bun! I'm stuck-- fast!

YEAH, I CAN *SEE.*

GOOD *LUCK* WITH THAT.

M-Mist--

Mister--

I'M PAULY FUCKING BRUCKNER! AND YOU'RE A MIDDLE-AGED WOMAN WITH A FACE LIKE A BABOON'S BUTT CRACK.

YOU JUST WROTE YOURSELF AS A GIRL BECAUSE YOU COULDN'T FACE WHAT YOU REALLY WERE!

OH, YES?

YOU'RE NOT AS CLEVER AS YOU THINK YOU ARE, MR. RABBIT.

NOT BY HALF.

FUCKING LET GO OF ME!

SOON. BUT IN THE MEANTIME--

--TELL ME WHAT YOU'RE DOING HERE.

NONE OF THIS WAS MY IDEA, YOU STUPID LITTLE BITCH!

WILSON TAYLOR STIFFED ME. I TRIED TO TAKE HIS MAP, AND THE NEXT THING I KNOW, I WAKE UP IN THE HUNDRED-ACRE GULAG!

NOT WHAT I MEANT. WHAT DID YOU COME TO THIS HOUSE FOR?

TODAY. NOW. WHAT IS IT THAT YOU WANT?

I TRIED TO ESCAPE A THOUSAND TIMES. NOTHING DOING.

THERE'S NOTHING PAST THE WOOD.

EXACTLY.

SO I THOUGHT--IF I KILL THE WRITER, MAYBE THE BUBBLE BURSTS.

LATERAL THINKING.

I HAVEN'T WRITTEN *ANYTHING* YET. I'M JUST A LITTLE GIRL.

*SURE* YOU ARE. WHATEVER WORKS FOR YOU.

NO. WHATEVER WORKS FOR THE *STORY.* I'M WHO I HAVE TO BE, TO MAKE IT COME OUT RIGHT.

EVERY STORY HAS A NEGATIVE SPACE, MISTER RABBIT.

THINGS IT CAN'T *ACKNOWLEDGE.* TRUTHS IT CAN IMPLY, OR FLIRT WITH, BUT NEVER SAY OUT *LOUD.*

RATCH

CLICK

DO I LOOK LIKE I *GIVE* A FLYING FUCK? LET ME GO!

ONE WAY OF WRITING FOR CHILDREN--*HER* WAY--IS TO TRY TO BE A CHILD YOURSELF.

AND THEN, IF YOU DO THAT... THE NEGATIVE SPACE IS *ENORMOUS.* GRIEF. PAIN. BETRAYAL. MORTALITY.

YOU HAVE TO PRETEND YOU DON'T *KNOW.*

TO *SUPPRESS* THE THINGS YOU LEARNED AS YOU GREW UP.

TO SLIP BACK INTO THE *GARDEN* BY BEING SMALL ENOUGH TO WALK UNDER THE DOOR.

BUT YOU CAN'T MAKE THE SCARY THINGS DISAPPEAR. YOU CAN ONLY LOCK THEM *AWAY* WHERE NOBODY SEES THEM.

AND UNCLE WILL GAVE ME THE KEY, TO KEEP IT SAFE UNTIL HE COMES BACK FOR IT.

NO FUCKING WAY.

WAY.

YEAH, BUT-- WHAT? A CELLAR FULL OF *GROWN-UPNESS*?

A CELLAR FULL OF THE *SINS* AND *SORROWS* OF THE WORLD.

YOU WANT *OUT,* MR. RABBIT?

ALL YOU EVER HAD TO DO WAS *ASK.*

And tumbly-twirly, head-over-heelsy, down he fell. A long, long way.

OW!

SHIT!

FUCK!

NUUH!

So far, he thought he'd never reach the bottom.

AWK!

THUD

But then he did.

FRIGGING LITTLE *SLAG.*

SRRRFFFF

IF I'D JUST AIMED AN INCH HIGHER...

FSSST...

YEARRRRRGGGGHHHHH!!

So Tig and Dogling went home.

And Tig said he believed it might be time for a little something.

And Dogling agreed that it very probably was.